10/07

FOCUS ON
FAMILY
MATTERS

# The Blending of Foster and Adopted Children into the Family

**FOCUS ON FAMILY MATTERS**

Focus on Family Matters

# The Blending of Foster and Adopted Children into the Family

Heather Lehr Wagner

Marvin Rosen, Ph.D.
Consulting Editor

Chelsea House Publishers
Philadelphia

**CHELSEA HOUSE PUBLISHERS**
EDITOR IN CHIEF  Sally Cheney
DIRECTOR OF PRODUCTION  Kim Shinners
CREATIVE MANAGER  Takeshi Takahashi
MANUFACTURING MANAGER  Diann Grasse

**Staff for THE BLENDING OF FOSTER AND ADOPTED CHILDREN INTO THE FAMILY**
ASSOCIATE EDITOR  Bill Conn
PICTURE RESEARCHER  Sarah Bloom
PRODUCTION ASSISTANT  Jaimie Winkler
SERIES DESIGNER  Takeshi Takahashi
LAYOUT  21st Century Publishing and Communications, Inc.

http://www.chelseahouse.com

First Printing

1 3 5 7 9 8 6 4 2

Library of Congress Cataloging-in-Publication Data

Wagner, Heather Lehr.
  The blending of foster and adopted children into the family / by Heather Lehr Wagner.
    p. cm. — (Focus on family matters)
Summary: Explores issues facing families confronting the challenges created by adoption
and foster care, and identifies steps members of blended families can take to ensure that
they have a strong foundation.
Includes bibliographical references and index.
  ISBN 0-7910-6694-0
  1. Stepfamilies—Juvenile literature.  2.  Foster parents—Juvenile literature.
[1. Stepfamilies.  2. Foster home care.  3. Family life.]  I. Title.  II. Series.
HQ759.92 .W335 2002
306.874—dc21
                                                                      2001008109

# Contents

# Introduction

**Marvin Rosen, Ph.D.**
Consulting Editor

B ad things sometimes happen to good people. We've prob-
ably all heard that expression. But what happens when the
"good people" are teenagers?

Growing up is stressful and difficult to negotiate. Teenagers
are struggling to becoming independent, trying to cut ties with
their families that they see as restrictive, burdensome, and
unfair. Rather than attempting to connect in new ways with
their parents, they may withdraw. When bad things do happen,
this separation may make the teen feel alone in coping with
difficult and stressful issues.

*Focus on Family Matters* provides teens with practical information about how to cope when bad things happen to them.
The series deals foremost with feelings—the emotional pain
associated with adversity. Grieving, fear, anger, stress, guilt,
and sadness are addressed head on. Teens will gain valuable
insight and advice about dealing with their feelings, and for
seeking help when they cannot help themselves.

The authors in this series identify some of the more serious
problems teens face. In so doing, they make three assumptions:
First, teens who find themselves in difficult situations are not at
fault and should not blame themselves. Second, teens can overcome difficult situations, but may need help to do so. Third,
teens bond with their families, and the strength of this bond
influences their ability to handle difficult situations.

These books are also about communication—specifically
about the value of communication. None of the problems
covered occurs in a vacuum, and none of the situations should

be faced by anyone alone. Each either involves a close family member or affects the entire family. Since families teach teens how to trust, relate to others, and solve problems, teens need to bond with families to develop normally and become emotionally whole. Success in dealing with adversity depends not only on the strength of the individual teen, but also upon the resources of the family in providing support, advice, and material assistance. Strong attachment to care givers in a supporting, nurturing, safe family structure is essential to successful coping.

Some teens learn to cope with adversity—they absorb the pain, they adjust, and they go on. But for others, the trauma they experience seems like an insurmountable challenge—they become angry, stressed, and depressed. They may withdraw from friends, they may stop going to school, and their grades may slip. They may draw negative attention to themselves and express their pain and fear by rebelling. Yet, in each case, healing can occur.

The teens who cope well with adversity, who are able to put the past behind them and regain their momentum, are no less sensitive or caring than those who suffer most. Yet there is a difference. Teens who are more resilient to trauma are able to dig deep down into their own resources, to find strength in their families and in their own skills, accomplishments, goals, aspirations, and values. They are able to find reasons for optimism and to feel confidence in their capabilities. This series recognizes the effectiveness of these strategies, and presents problem-solving skills that every teen can use.

*Focus on Family Matters* is positive, optimistic, and supportive. It gives teens hope and reinforces the power of their own efforts to handle adversity. And most importantly, it shows teens that while they cannot undo the bad things that have happen, they have the power to shape their own futures and flourish as healthy, productive adults.

# The Challenges for Adopted and Foster Families

■ Danielle considered herself lucky. She had been "chosen," her parents had told her over and over again. They had waited and hoped for her, year after year. Until finally, in an act of great generosity, her birth mother had given her life—and then given her a life with these parents, in this place. The fact that she had been adopted had always been clear and known to her, as much a part of her sense of self as the town she lived in or her last name. But still, she couldn't help feeling as if a part of her was missing, as if her life was a puzzle that still needed to be solved. She was athletic, a "total jock," as her friends said, and her parents were hopeless at any kind of sport. She had a strong, clear singing voice, and neither her mother nor father could carry a tune. Her hair was reddish blonde, her eyes turquoise. Where had all of that come from? Was there a mother or father somewhere who looked like her? Did she have a brother or sister? And, most important, why had she been given away for someone else to love and raise?

**All children struggle with asserting their independence and forming their own identity. These issues can be especially challenging for adopted and foster children who may have unanswered questions about their birth parents.**

All teenagers struggle with feeling different from other members of their family, and with trying to become independent from their parents while building their own identity. But for those who have joined a family as adopted or foster children, the challenges are even greater. Their sense of connection is weaker and constantly being tested. Even in relatively happy situations, there is an ongoing mystery that demands to be solved: Where did I come from? Who are my "real" parents? Why did they give me away?

## Adoption: the basics

In an **adoption**, a parent or parents are given the legal right to raise a child as their own, even though they are not the natural parents of that child. Adoptions may occur through many different sources: a child may be adopted by a stepparent or relative; he or she may be adopted following time in foster care; a child from another country may be adopted by a U.S. family; or adoptions may be handled through a private agency or independent person such as a lawyer.

**What happens in an adoption?**

Because of the variety of forms of adoption and ways in which they can take place, it is difficult to find specific statistics showing exactly how many adoptions take place in a given year. However, estimates generally show that approximately 125,000 children are adopted each year in the U.S.

Adoption can be an expensive and time-consuming process. The cost of an adoption is generally $10,000 to $20,000, and parents may wait for several years to adopt a healthy American infant. As a result, more Americans who are eager to adopt are turning overseas, to adopt needy children from other countries. While adoptees come from many different parts of the world, the largest number of children adopted from other countries come from Russia, China, Korea, and Guatemala.

There are many accomplished and successful adults who were once adopted. Actors Halle Berry and Ray Liotta, and singers Faith Hill and Sarah McLachlan, were adopted. Several of the world's greatest writers, including Louisa May Alcott, Charles Dickens, and Mark Twain, were adopted. Athletes

> **What makes being adopted so difficult?**

like Surya Bonaly, Eric Dickerson, Scott Hamilton, and Mark Acre began their lives as adopted children. Influential civil rights activists like Malcolm X and Jesse Jackson, international leaders like Nelson Mandela, even the famed inventor George Washington Carver—all were adopted. Two adoptees even grew up to be Presidents of the United States: Gerald Ford and Bill Clinton.

## What is a foster family?

If you look up the word "foster" in the dictionary, you will see that it means to help something grow or develop. **Foster parents** do this for their **foster children**—they give them a safe place to live, sometimes for a day or two, sometimes for much longer. Children are placed with a foster family when their own parents are unable to care for them. An official from the state government will step in and find a family who can help these children until their parents are able to take care of them again.

A child might be placed with a **foster family** if his or her parents are very sick, abusing drugs, in jail, or if there is violence in the home. The goal of foster care is to give the parents a chance to focus on their own lives for a while, to sort out their own problems so that they can then take care of their children and concentrate on what their children need.

**Sometimes a child is placed in foster care for his or her own safety. If a child's birth parents are violent or addicted to drugs, a court or agency may place the child with foster parents who can provide a safer place to live for a short period of time.**

It can be very difficult for children placed in foster families. They may have to be separated not only from their parents, but also from their brothers and sisters, as foster families seldom can take care of more than one child. They may have to change schools, and adjust to living in a new place with new family members. They often remain with a foster family for only a short time, so they may have to move more than once before they are reunited with their **birth parents** or adopted.

## What is the difference

**between an adopted family and a foster family?**

In the following chapters, we will explore the issues facing families who are confronted with the challenges created by adoption and foster care. We will discuss the concerns adopted children have, and how best to handle them. We will talk about the pros and cons of searching for birth parents, and how and where to begin that search. We will explore the situation facing foster children and their families, and examine the obstacles they face in their efforts to build a home together. Most importantly, we will think about the steps adoptive and foster families can take to ensure that they *are* a family, strong and secure in their foundation.

# Being Adopted

■ Unlike some adopted children who know nothing of their birth parents, Ed knew a few details about his birth mother. She was only 15 years old when she became pregnant, she wasn't married, and had no one to help her raise a child. Ed had thought about his birth mother a lot, and understood why she had given him up for adoption. By doing so she gave him a better life with his adoptive parents than she could ever have provided.

Still, Ed wondered what his birth mother was doing now. Did she have other children and a family of her own? Did she ever think about him? Did she have any desire to get to know him or more about his life?

If you are adopted, there is at least one day each year when you become painfully aware of what makes you different: your birthday. While other families may share funny stories about the date—an unexpected rush to the hospital, a child born two weeks later than expected or on a

**Birthdays can be a difficult time for adopted children. They may wonder about their birth parents, where they live, why they put their child up for adoption, and whether or not they remember their child's birthday. Confronting these feelings can be difficult, and it is important to share them with adoptive parents and friends.**

holiday or in the middle of the night—the facts surrounding an adopted child's birth are often mysterious and unknown. A birthday can become yet another painful reminder of what is missing—details, facts, and information about the day your life began.

A birthday can cause you to think about your birth

mother and wonder what the day meant for her. Was she sad that she had to give you away? Had she decided by then that she would place you with another family? Was she frightened or upset? Did she hold you after you were born? These questions are all normal and natural. It is equally normal, on your birthday, to wonder whether, somewhere, your birth mother is remembering the day and thinking about you.

Parents who adopt children frequently describe them as special because they have been hoped for and, ultimately, "chosen." But most adopted teens feel that there are two parts to the process of being adopted—being wanted by their adopted parents, but also not being wanted by their birth parents. Many adopted children remember this as a particularly painful point in their life—the day when they understood that their adoption depended on someone (their birth parent) not wanting them.

**What question**

**would you most want your birth mother to answer?**

Of course, the decisions leading up to an adoption are generally more complicated. Many birth parents love their children, but because of circumstances (their age, their financial situation, or pressure from family members) they are unable to care for their child, to give it the best possible life. They choose to give a child up for adoption in the sincere hope that another family will give their child a good life, better than the one they could offer.

## Who could give up their baby?

Many teens—and some adults, as well—struggle with the question of why a parent would choose to give their child up for adoption. As mentioned earlier, it is never an easy choice. An unplanned pregnancy may be one reason—a young, unmarried mother may understand that she is unable to take care of a child financially or emotionally. Family pressure may be another reason. Today it is more common to see single women raising children, but 10 to 15 years ago, this was not the case and being an unmarried mother was much more difficult in American society. A birth mother may believe

**What would make you** choose to place your child for adoption?

that a married couple will be better able to provide for her child, both in terms of offering a stable, loving home and by knowing that the child will have two parents to care for him or her.

In some cases, children are placed in foster care or with an adopted family when the parents have died, or are unable to care for their children. Parents may be unable to raise their children because of their own extreme poverty, poor health, addictions, or mental disease. It is important to remember that each time an adopted or foster child wonders why their parents made this choice, the answer is almost always because they believed it would be the best for their child.

## How it feels to be adopted

Adoption can take many different forms, and so the feelings that go with being adopted are quite different, too. For many adopted children, the feeling they talk about often is a sense of being incomplete. It can feel as if you are trying to put together a puzzle—the puzzle of who you are—and there are several pieces missing.

It is normal to have questions about your birth parents. Where do they live? What do they do? Do they have other

**Many factors influence the decision to adopt a child, and adoptive parents may not be comfortable discussing these issues with their children until they feel they are old enough to understand. It is important for adopted children to ask their adoptive parents questions, and equally important to be patient while waiting for the answers.**

children now? What do they look like? Could they be someone famous? And, of course, do they think about me?

If you find yourself wrestling with these kinds of questions, spending a lot of time wondering or worrying about your birth parents, you may find it helpful to put your questions down on paper. You may want to keep a journal, recording your thoughts. Some adopted children imagine that they are writing a letter to their birth mother or birth parents, placing on paper the questions they would like to someday have answered.

You may ask your parents for any information they feel comfortable sharing about your adoption—the details they know about your birth, the events surrounding your adoption, or any facts they can provide. Eventually, you may wish to search for your birth parents. This process will be discussed further in a later chapter.

For many young teens, adoption can be something that makes you different at a time when you most want to fit in with your friends. Friends may talk about looking like their mother or father; a science class on genetics explores how things like eye color and height are passed from parent to child. There are many times when you may feel uncomfortable or even angry about being adopted. Some families are more open in discussing the adoption than others—for some it may be an event to be celebrated as a day that the family became complete, for others it may be something to be avoided.

The remarks of strangers can often be another opportunity for embarrassment or discomfort. Someone may comment on how different your appearance is from your parents, or may ask you a question about your **ethnic background** or heritage. Children adopted

**Would you let** people know that you were adopted, or keep it a secret?

from other countries must often deal with thoughtless comments or questions, all of which can make you feel as if you are defined by your adoption rather than by who you are as a person.

It can be helpful to remember that your birth would ultimately bring great joy to your adopted parents. If you do not know the details of how you came to become part of your family, ask your parents to share as much as they can. Ask about the process of your adoption—how they found you, what the adoption involved step-by-step, what your first day with the family was like. Ask them to share their feelings about your adoption. Understanding what it was like for them should help you to know how special your birth was for them.

The experience of being adopted is unique and unlike any other. You may find yourself struggling with feelings of anger, depression, or fear. We will explore some practical ways to deal with these feelings in the last chapter of this book.

## Who chooses to adopt

Each adoption is a complicated story, nearly all beginning and ending with a loving adult wanting to give a child the very best life possible. For parents, the decision to adopt a child can result from many different factors. A couple may be unable to have a biological child for physical reasons, and yet long to be parents. They may decide to adopt because they learn of a child that needs a caring home. A single man or woman may wish to share his or her home and life with a child. In some cases, a stepparent or family member chooses to adopt a child when one or both biological parents are unable to care for the child.

The statistics show that there are five to six parents wishing to adopt for every child that is adopted. The process can take several years, and is quite expensive, as we discussed in the first chapter. There are many different ways that parents go about adopting a child. They may use a religious agency, a

**Would you choose to adopt a child?**

private adoption agency, or a government organization that places children with foster or adoptive families. They may arrange a **private adoption**, where an attorney, doctor, or other contact provides them with the details of a child awaiting adoption.

Adoptive parents are generally screened very carefully to ensure that they can provide a good home for the child. They are often visited by an adoption agency representative to see what kind of home they can provide. They are asked many questions, and required to give extensive medical information to make sure that they are healthy and able to be good parents. In the case of international adoptions, parents must frequently meet guidelines set by their state government, their national government, and the requirements of the country from which they are adopting.

It is clear from all of this that adopted children should view themselves as "chosen." Their birth parents have chosen to give them a better life than they believed they could provide. Their adopted parents have chosen to wait, to hope, to undertake the expense and effort, to answer the questions and provide the necessary information to show that they will be good parents. And the adoption agency or representative has chosen them and their adopted parents to be a family.

It is also clear that an adopted child is part of a circle of loving adults who have helped shape that family. This circle includes the birth parents, the adopted parents, and the agency or organization that helped match child and family. For some children adopted from another country, the circle stretches around the world. For others, the borders are more narrow. But in every case, the circle would not exist without the child at its center.

Fitting in with friends is important to every teenager, and adoption may make a teen feel different at this crucial stage of life. Adopted children should remember that they were chosen by their adoptive parents, and will always have their support as they face the challenges of growing up.

## The last word

At the moment when you most want to feel like everyone else, being adopted can separate you from your friends. It can be something "different," and give you a feeling of not belonging. It can make it even harder to communicate with your parents, and cause you to believe that somewhere there is a mother and father who would understand you better and love you more.

There are resources that can help—books that may be useful, web sites that may provide you with a useful network of teens wrestling with similar issues and looking for some of the same answers you are. We will list them at the end of this book.

# Who Am I?

■ Donna was adopted from China, and her adoptive parents are Caucasian. She never really thought about how she looked standing next to her parents until one parent-teacher night at her school. John, a Chinese boy in her class, asked her why her parents didn't look like her, why her hair was straight and black while her mom's was curly and blonde.

Donna couldn't find out anything about her birth parents, so she decided to learn about her Chinese heritage. She asked John many questions about his family, found information on the Internet, and she and her parents went to Chinatown with John's family to celebrate the Chinese New Year. It was so exciting and different, and made Donna want to know all about Chinese culture.

The question "Who am I?" is common to all adopted children. All feel placed—by grace or chance—with a group of strangers who have become their family. Some

**All adopted children question their identity and wonder who they are and where they came from. These children will have to ask a lot of questions and be willing to share their feelings with family and friends to find out about their lives before the adoption.**

children, adopted as toddlers or older children, still hold on to memories of their life before they were adopted.

For children adopted from other countries, or of a racial background different from that of their adoptive parents, the question can become not simply "*Who* am I?" but also "*What* am I?" Adopted children feel different as it is. It can be even more challenging when you are the only African-American person in your school, or the only Asian person in your neighborhood. When your physical appearance is noticeably different from that of your parents, the fact that you are adopted can be obvious even to strangers.

As a teenager, you are struggling to build your own identity, to get a sense of who you are as an individual, apart from your family. When you must gain a greater sense of your own racial or ethnic identity at the same time, adolescence can become a real struggle.

## Interracial adoption

Why are adopted children sometimes placed with a family of a different race? The vast majority of families hoping to adopt a child are white. While this fact is changing slightly, it still remains true that more white parents are available for adopted children than minority parents. As a result, while race may be one factor in deciding who would best be able to parent a child, other factors must also be considered.

### Have you ever

experienced prejudice because of your race or ethnic background?

Approximately eight percent of adoptions are **transracial** or **transethnic** (where children are of a different race or ethnic background than their adoptive parents); approximately one percent of all adoptions involve African-American children adopted by white parents. For adults anxious to provide a home for a child, the fact that the child may be of a different race or heritage is often not a significant factor. Their definition of family may not be limited by appearance or culture or anything that came "before." For them, the family begins with the adoption and its members are held together by the adoption.

Unfortunately, life is not always so neat and simple for the adopted children. Even under the best of circumstances, schools consist of many small groups, cliques, and clubs.

Students group themselves—or are grouped by their peers—according to their interests, their athletic abilities, their intelligence, their clothes, and their appearance. When this division extends to race, children whose race differs from that of their adoptive parents can find themselves in a kind of "no-man's land." An African-American teen may find himself or herself labeled "black" by white peers, yet "not black enough" by other African-Americans.

Most teens struggle with the sense that their parents don't understand them. When parents have adopted a minority child, this sense of miscommunication and lack of understanding can be magnified. Prejudice is still a real and terrible fact in our society, and minorities are subjected to a different experience—an experience that can be nearly impossible for white parents of a minority child to appreciate.

Of course, for all of us, it is important to have a real and strong sense of "belonging," whether in our schools, with our friends, or with our family. Families can offer a strong anchor point, and for those children fortunate enough to live in a home where there is support for exploring other cultures and heritages, it can be helpful to seek out ways to explore more details of your ethnic identity.

There are many organizations and resources designed to provide information that will be helpful to young people of particular racial or ethnic backgrounds. Some of them are listed at the end of this book.

## International adoptions

In the case of **international adoptions**, information about your heritage can be quite sketchy. It is often almost impossible to obtain any details about an adoption from overseas sources, where different regulations govern adoption agencies. And so you are often left with a

**With international adoptions, it may be difficult to obtain accurate information about birth parents. Information sources like libraries and the Internet can help adopted children learn about their culture and heritage.**

question mark, an empty place where you should have a clear sense of who you are.

Even if you are unable to obtain details about your biological parents, you may find it helpful to begin to look for cultural or racial information, details that will provide you with information about your heritage on a larger scale. The Internet can be a good starting point for learning more information—you may want to research information about your place of birth, or look at a local newspaper from your country of origin. You may wish to find a CD of music from your native country, or listen (via the Internet) to a radio station from that country.

Some organizations sponsor culture clubs or culture camps —places where children from a particular ethnic background can come together. It can be a

> **What part of your**
>
> **heritage or background is most important to you?**

wonderful experience for teens to be surrounded by others with similar stories or questions. There are culture camps or clubs for children adopted from China, Vietnam, India, Russia, and the Ukraine. This is only the beginning. There are many other organizations that strive to provide support and a greater sense of community for children adopted from other countries—and their families. A list of web sites with information of interest to children and teens adopted from overseas appears at the back of this book.

## Creating a life book

A **life book** may be a useful way to begin the process of understanding your life—of moving beyond the question "What am I?" to being able to answer the question "Who am I?"

Some adoptive parents prepare life books for their adopted children to help hold together the pieces of their life that led up to the adoption. If you do not yet have this valuable book, you may wish to begin to assemble one yourself. A life book is exactly what it sounds like—the story of your life, a way to assemble the facts, the background, and the events that made you who you are today.

Much like your life, a life book will not be created in a day, nor should it have an ending. You are the reporter, noting down the important details that make up your life story. Include whatever matters to you; share it with others or keep

# To Search or Not to Search

On Megan's 16th birthday, she decided that she wanted to find her birth mother. Although she considered her adoptive parents to be her "real" parents, she had so many questions to ask her birth mother, like why she was given up for adoption. Megan was afraid to ask her parents to help her search for her birth mother, because she thought it might hurt their feelings or make them feel like she didn't love them.

Once she got up enough courage, she did ask them for help. Her adoptive parents told Megan that they had expected her to want to search, and that they would give her their full support. The next day, Megan and her parents began the search by calling the adoption agency that arranged her adoption.

For many children who have been adopted, the decision to search for a birth parent can be a difficult and painful one. It is natural to feel connected to your birth parent, and to want to know that person. The process of your birth and adoption

**Adopted children have many questions about their birth parents. Deciding whether to search for their birth family is a difficult decision they should make with the guidance and support of adoptive parents.**

can feel almost like a mystery—a mystery that you want to solve. A fundamental question—"Why was I given up for adoption?"—can demand to be answered. And often a birth parent is the only person who can provide that answer.

For those who have not been adopted, it can be hard to understand why this question is so important. And yet even if you have been adopted into a loving, wonderful family, it can still be frustrating to feel that there is a connection with someone else, someone unknown who may look like you, share the same talents, and be related to you in the most basic way.

The question "Why?" is common to all people who learn that they have been adopted. But for teens, the challenges posed by adoption can be especially great, and the need for answers can be particularly strong. The teenage years are a time when you begin to shape your own identity, separate from that of your family. You begin to make your own choices—or at least want to make more of your own choices!—recognizing that your tastes in clothes, music, and even food may now be quite different from that of your parents.

**Why would someone who has been adopted want to find his or her birth parents?**

Part of the process of shaping your own identity involves thinking about your parents, and modeling yourself after them in certain ways, but not in others. You may admire the fact that your mother worked, and choose to have a career like hers. You may appreciate the fact that your family was small (or large) and plan to have a similar number of children. You may hate the fact that your father had to work every weekend, and vow not to take a job that requires such long hours. Each of these decisions is the result of watching, studying, and absorbing the life of your family and accepting or rejecting bits and pieces of it. It is as if your future is a puzzle that you are putting together slowly, checking each piece to see what fits.

For adopted teens, the puzzle feels more complicated

since certain pieces are missing. As you grow older, you may begin to think about your birth parents in new ways. You may wonder how old your birth mother was when you were born. You may wonder where she lived, and where she is now. You may wonder if there are brothers or sisters somewhere, or pass someone on the street and wonder if they could be a relative.

## Should you search?

It is important to remember that a decision about whether or not to search for your birth parents should be made only after long and careful thought. It should never be done out of anger or disappointment. It is tempting to believe that finding your birth mother or birth parents will solve all problems, or that they will somehow treat you better than your adopted parents. This is, of course, not realistic.

If you find yourself asking, "Who are my *real* parents?" you should remember that a parent is someone who cares for and raises their children. The parents who adopted you, who took care of you and loved you as you grew, are your *real* parents. They may feel anxious or uncomfortable at the prospect of you looking for your birth parents. They may feel rejected, or believe that they are not good enough.

You will need their support and understanding if you decide to search for your birth parents. It is important to discuss your plans honestly and openly with them, to give everyone an opportunity to share their concerns and to work together.

## Telling your parents

Parents who have not been adopted themselves may struggle with their child's decision to search for a birth parent. They may already be finding it difficult to deal with their child growing up. They may already be feeling rejected as their children turn more to peers than to their parents in shaping their interests. This may feel like yet another rejection—and this time, to another parent!

But is this a reason to avoid telling your parents? Absolutely not. It is important for your parents to understand your questions and to support you in finding the answers. And it is equally important for you to let them know that you value their support and understanding as you search.

For this reason, it is helpful for you to be clear about the reasons why you want to find your birth parent. You may want to make a list of questions you have, questions that only your birth parent can answer. Be specific, and make the list as long as you like. Your list may contain questions like these:

**What facts about your birth are the most important for you to know?**

- How old was my birth mother when I was born?
- What was her relationship with my birth father?
- Why did she decide to give me up for adoption?
- What does she remember about the day I was born?
- Who do I look like?
- Are there any health problems in my birth family that are important for me to know?
- Do I have any brothers or sisters?
- Where does my talent for [swimming, singing, football, etc.] come from?

If you are of a different race or ethnic background than your adopted parents, there may be additional questions that you would like to have answered—questions about culture, heritage, or religion.

A detailed list will help you when you explain the search to your parents. With a list of clear and specific questions, the reasons for your search are much easier for others to understand.

Your adoptive parents may feel reluctant for you to undertake this search, even if your relationship with them is strong and you have reassured them of your love. They may feel that you should wait until you are an adult before beginning the search, fearing that the emotions the search will bring to the surface may be overwhelming. The most important thing is to communicate—let them know your reasons for searching and listen to their reasons for urging you to wait. In general, records may not be available to teens until they are adults, so if your parents are not supportive it may make sense to postpone the search, until they feel more comfortable with you undertaking the process.

Fear can often play a large part in the initial discussions with your adopted parents. You may fear their reaction to your desire to search for your birth parents; they may fear that they will somehow be replaced by another "real" parent. In nearly every case, however, the search process can strengthen the relationship among adopted family members. The process of searching, when supported and understood, creates a new bond—one that can not be replaced, regardless of the search's outcome.

You may also find that an honest discussion of your wish to search makes it easier to discuss the adoption itself. For many families, an adoption is a forbidden topic, something to be ignored, as if the adoption will somehow weaken the family bonds. Again, honesty is critical. The process of discussing the search may make it easier for everyone to talk about the adoption itself, opening new doors to better communication in general.

## Beginning the search

The first source of information about birth parents can come from your adopted parents—another reason why it is important to be open and honest with them about your

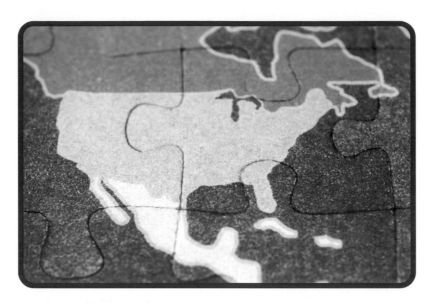

**The search for birth parents can seem like a complex puzzle with many missing pieces and unanswered questions. This task is more manageable with information from adoptive parents, and a clear idea of what the adopted or foster child hopes to gain by finding the birth parents.**

plans. They may know small pieces of information that can help begin the search in a more specific fashion—details about the religion or ethnic background of birth parents, information about where the adoption took place, and details about the hospital or city where you were born.

Since adoption records are frequently sealed, these small bits of information can be quite valuable and useful, both in answering some basic questions and in planning out a search. There are groups located throughout the country that specialize in helping adopted children find birth parents, and birth parents find children given up for adoption. As a teenager, you will need your parent's permission to join one of these groups, but you may find them a useful source both of support and resources.

If an agency handled your adoption, that agency will have

certain information available, known as **non-identifying information**. These are basic facts that will not give you your birth mother's name or address, but may provide information about your birth mother's health, what she looked like, her religion, educational background, job, or some basic details about the adoption.

## Making contact

When your search results in finding your birth mother, what comes next? It is important to be prepared for many different possibilities—yet another reason why your search should always begin with the support of your parents or other caring friends and adults who can help you plan how to handle contact with birth parents.

> **What would you want** to ask your birth mother when you contacted her for the first time?

It is critical to remember that, for many birth parents, the decision to give a child up for adoption was undoubtedly a difficult and painful one. They may have felt guilt or sadness about their choice. They may have been embarrassed at an unplanned pregnancy or saddened by a relationship that was unable to support a child. For these and other reasons, a birth parent may be unable or unwilling to immediately begin a relationship with the child they gave up for adoption. A phone call "out of the blue" can be a painful reminder of a difficult time. They will not always have had the time to prepare for contact with the child, and their initial reaction to this contact can be awkward, or even angry.

They may have married or had other children, without sharing the details of their earlier pregnancy. Unless the birth parent, too, has been searching, any initial contact will catch them by surprise, particularly if they believed that their records were sealed and information unavailable.

Should you decide to contact your birth parent, it is important to be prepared for many different reactions and have a plan should the call or contact not go as well as you may have hoped. For many reasons, a letter may be an easier initial contact than a phone call. It will give the birth parent a chance to think about whether or not they wish to have contact, and also give them an opportunity to find a place and time where a conversation might be comfortable.

> **If you had given** a child up for adoption, what kind of a relationship would you want to have with that child after the adoption?

Just as you need to be prepared for many different reactions and emotions from your birth parent, you should also be prepared for a wide range of emotions in yourself. When your search ends in successfully locating your birth parent, you may feel first joy, and then fear, and ultimately anger. The strength of their anger often catches adopted children by surprise. Finally being able to speak with your birth parent, and get answers to the questions that have troubled you for so long, can be overwhelming. This is yet another reason why it is important for you to have the support of your parents or other caring adults throughout your search.

## A final thought

For many adopted children, struggling with a sense that their adopted parents don't really understand them, there can be an unrealistic expectation that their birth parents will. But a birth parent and his or her child, separated by time and distance, are strangers, and any relationship will take time to grow. It is unrealistic to imagine that life will become much better once you find your birth parent or parents.

Adoption is both the beginning and the ending of the

**The search for birth parents can sometimes leave an adopted child feeling alone and confused. Adopted children should remember that a parent is someone who gives love and guidance to their children, and that their adoptive parents have always provided these necessities.**

story. Locating your birth mother may provide answers and information. But it will not change the fact of your adoption. Nor will it change who you are. You are more than a birth certificate, more than the place where you were born or the events that brought you into the world. Before beginning any search, you should be clear and realistic about what you want to learn. Finding a birth parent may reveal the earliest moments of your life. But it will not tell you who you are. Those answers must come from you.

# Fostering a Family

■ Missy could clearly remember her mother, but she had not seen her for a long time. Her mother had been addicted to drugs, and sometimes she would drink too much, and so one day two people came and took Missy and her brothers and sisters away. Each of them had gone to a different place. Missy had lived with three different families since that day they took her away from her home. But she believed that, one day, her family would come back together. Her mother would be well and healthy, and she and her brothers and sisters would have their home again. For now, she moved from place to place. Some people she lived with were kind, others didn't even seem to know she was there. One woman had been very mean. But none of them called her their daughter. None of them considered her a part of their family. She was introduced as "the foster girl," as if she didn't exist except as someone apart from the rest of the family. Missy told herself it didn't matter. They weren't really her family, anyway. Her real family was out there, and one day they would be together again.

**Foster care offers a child a safe place to live when their own family environment is unhealthy or unstable. Unlike a permanent adoption, foster care is designed as a temporary solution to a difficult situation.**

The needs and concerns of children in foster care are quite different from those of children who have been adopted, and so this chapter will focus specifically on questions about foster families. As we have discussed earlier, the word foster means to care for someone, to nurture them and help them grow. A child is placed in a foster family because his or her birth parents are unable to care for their child, either because of a physical or mental illness, because there has been a concern about abuse, because the parents may be battling addictions to drugs or alcohol, or for some other specific reason. Generally, these placements are intended to be temporary—the child is put with a family who can help care for him or her until the parents are once again able to care for their child.

Each state has different types, or stages, of foster care, but in general foster care can be divided into five categories:

- *Emergency foster care*: a sudden and unexpected problem in the home has made it difficult for parents to take care of their child. The child will be placed with a foster family, but for no more than 30 days.

- *Limited foster care*: foster care is to be temporary, but the time frame for the child returning to his or her family is not yet known.

- *Pre-adoptive foster care*: a child is placed in foster care until he or she can be adopted. This generally happens when it is determined that a child can not return to his or her birth parents.

- *Permanent foster care*: if there are some special circumstances that prevent a child from being adopted, a child may be placed in permanent foster care. Today, more agencies are working to avoid this stage, so that children can be adopted if necessary.

- *Specialized foster care*: this type of foster care is for children who are seriously ill, handicapped, or part of a family of children that should be placed as a group rather than one by one.

As these types of foster care make clear, a foster family is in most cases intended to be a temporary solution to a difficult family situation, a way to ensure that children are cared for on a short-term basis until a permanent conclusion (adoption or returning the child to his or her birth family) can be reached. Unfortunately, foster care often becomes long-term rather than temporary, creating problems rather than solving them.

**Why is a child placed with a foster family?**

Many children placed in foster care move from one foster family to another while agencies attempt to resolve the problems that put them in foster care in the first place. They generally have trouble connecting with their foster family, particularly if they have lived with several different families in a relatively short period of time. It may be more difficult for them to trust, to become attached and involved with other people, or to form relationships with others. The average child placed in foster care will be away from his or her parents for more than two years, and in that time half of all foster children will live in at least two different foster homes. As a short-term solution, it can be helpful to have a safe place where a child can live until a more permanent place can be found. It is when foster care becomes a long-term place-ment that children suffer.

## Becoming a foster family

Foster parents are generally people who want to help needy children. Adults may care for a number of foster children, and so the shape and scope of the foster family can change as children come and go. Foster parents may become particularly good at caring for a special-needs child, for example, so that several physically challenged or mentally handicapped children may be placed in the same family. This can provide an opportunity for children, at a difficult crossroads in their life, to at least be in a group of children who are struggling with some of the same challenges and problems.

**Children in foster care face some hard questions that may challenge their ideas about trust and permanence. Children may even make the mistake of blaming themselves for being separated from their birth parents.**

Foster parents are given financial assistance to care for foster children, so some adults may choose to become foster parents if they wish to help care for children but are unable to afford all of the expenses involved in adopting or raising children. However, the money provided is generally limited, certainly not enough for foster parenting to become a kind of business or money-making operation.

In some cases, a child may be placed with a foster family as a first step toward adoption. In these families, a child comes to live with a family as an initial stage. If all goes well, if the child is comfortable in the family and if the parents feel that they can adequately care and provide for the child, the child may ultimately be adopted by the foster parents.

For a child or teenager placed in foster care, there are a number of very difficult questions with which he or she must wrestle. Can I trust my foster parents? Am I somehow to blame for the events that brought me to this foster family? Will I ever go back to my family? Why haven't my parents been able to come and get me?

These questions are complex ones, and they are made more complicated by the fact that a child comes into a foster family because of some serious problems in the birth family. Most often it is because the parents have either abused or neglected their children (meaning that they have not properly cared for their children—making sure that they have enough to eat, are safe and clothed, that they go to school, and all of the other critical steps in parenting).

Even when parents have not cared for their child, they are often unwilling to allow the child to be adopted by another adult who is in a position to provide the necessary care. This is why some children spend too much time in the foster care system, moving from one family to another. They may be placed with a family for a short period of time, in the hope that their birth parent will take steps to correct the problems that caused the child to be placed in foster care in the first place. A birth parent may not be willing or able to admit that they can not control their addiction or get the kind of help necessary to ensure that the abuse or neglect does not happen again. They may sincerely hope that their family will be reunited one day, but yet not be able to make that happen. For these and many

**Are children in foster care ever returned to their birth families?**

other reasons, birth parents may be willing to allow their children to remain in foster care, rather than permitting them to be adopted.

## Feelings in a foster family

A foster family faces very special challenges. If you are living in a foster family, you may naturally hope that you will once more be with your birth parent or birth parents some day. You may not clearly remember the circumstances that brought you to the foster family, or you may wish to wipe them away and so choose not to remember what your life was really like. You will feel angry at times—angry at everyone: your birth parents for not being able to bring you home, and your foster parents for not being your birth parents. If there are other children in your foster family, you will no doubt feel angry at them.

If you have moved from one foster home to another, it can be quite difficult to accept that you are living as a *family*. A family should be a stable and permanent group of people who have been joined together—in foster care, it may seem that you just begin to feel "at home" in one place when you are moved to another.

If there are other children in the family, either adopted or birth children, foster children often feel that they are treated differently. They may feel that the foster parents favor their "real" children, or hear comments from the family's friends and relatives that place them in a separate category, as if they were guests or worse.

**What would it feel like** to move from one place to another, without knowing when you will return to your home?

Foster care, even with its goal of temporary placement and the reunion of families, may make it more difficult for families to maintain contact in some cases. Brothers and sisters may not always be placed in the same family; birth parents may not be given information about the foster family with which their child is living; and children may see or speak with their birth parents only infrequently, if ever. It can be shattering to know that other family members are somewhere, perhaps nearby, and yet be unable to see them or spend time with them.

Often it is difficult to know exactly how long a foster placement will last. This can be the most frustrating aspect of life in a foster family. For anyone, moving from one place to another can be difficult, sad, and frightening. Imagine how it would feel to move from one family to another to another, never knowing when or if you would be reunited with your birth family.

Adjusting to a foster family is difficult. Each foster family will have different rules, different beliefs and values, perhaps be of a different religion, or be in a place that requires you to attend a different school. It is impossible to overstate how traumatic it can be to make this move and adjust to a new family's rules and attitudes, only to have to move again. To lose your home and family is upsetting enough. With each new move, it can become increasingly impossible to feel "at home" anywhere.

There are approximately half a million U.S. children in the foster care system. It is no surprise that many of them are struggling with emotional illnesses, poverty, and a future that is more difficult than for children who have been adopted or are living with their birth parents. As the children grow older, many of them will be placed in residential treatment facilities to help them cope with a wide range of issues.

It is a bleak future and one that requires tremendous strength and support to overcome. Some children will be fortunate enough to be placed in a foster family that provides love and encouragement, that treats them kindly

**Of the nearly half million foster children in the United States, many come from homes affected by poverty, emotional illness, or abuse. With the right coping skills and the support of their foster families, these children can turn a difficult past into a future with promise.**

and yet understands their wish to return home. Others will not be so lucky. Foster children almost universally dream of the day when they can return to their home, no matter how difficult the situation may have been there. Sadly, that dream does not always come true.

The foster family faces a particular challenge as it blends together different members with different needs. Foster parents wish to create a home, to provide structure, to set rules and to care for children in what they believe is the best way possible. Foster children will, in almost all cases, wish to be returned to their birth family. Is it possible to create a family under these conditions?

The answer is yes, provided that at the outset, all members of the foster family treat each other fairly and with respect. Foster parents should understand the responsibility they have been given, not simply to take care of children but to love them and nurture them. They should be willing to respect the importance of the birth parents to their children, even if they do not agree with how they chose to care for their children. They should do their best to understand the "before" for their foster child—what his or her life was like before they became a part of the foster family—in order to better care for each member of the new family.

Foster children can take some measure of control, as well. They must first understand clearly that they are in no way responsible for the circumstances that placed them in foster care. Their actions, their behavior, their words, were not the cause of the breakdown in their family, nor will their behavior be able to correct the circumstances. Some foster children incorrectly believe that if they are good enough, if they work hard enough, they will be "rewarded" by being returned to their birth family. This is, of course, not the case, since it was the inability of their parents to properly care for them that brought them to a foster family in the first place. It will be up to their birth parents to change those circumstances in order to reunite the family once more.

Does this mean that foster children are helpless? No. They have a responsibility to themselves, to be healthy, to survive and even thrive, to be honest about their feelings and learn how to manage them in a way that will help them go on to a better life. In the next chapter, we will explore the ways in which both foster and adopted children can deal with their emotions and feelings in a positive, healthy way.

# Dealing with Feelings

■ For Tim, the news that he had been adopted had come as a shock. He had been 10 when he found out. Although several years had passed since the day his mother and father revealed this piece of his past, he still felt it keenly, as if someone had punched him in the stomach and he couldn't catch his breath. It had made everything about his life seem false. What else were they hiding, these people who had pretended to be his parents for all those years? Worse still, Tim learned that his younger brother was not adopted, but had been born to his parents one year after he came to live with them. It had always seemed to Tim that his parents treated his younger brother differently, as if they loved him more. Now he understood why. His brother was their "real" son. Tim found himself constantly fighting with his younger brother, with his parents, and getting into trouble at school. He was thinking about running away. This wasn't really his home.

**Both adopted and foster children must face painful feelings of isolation, guilt, and anger. Coping with these feelings when they arise is an important key to overcoming future problems and building healthy relationships.**

As we have discussed in previous chapters, adopted and foster children struggle with many different feelings, most of which are quite difficult for those not in their situation to understand. Adopted children may feel different from their friends at school when discussions about family roots or resemblances come up. Foster children may feel permanently unsettled and unable to feel at home anywhere, always waiting for the next move, always hoping to return to their birth family. Adopted children may wrestle with guilt when they feel a desire to find out about their birth mother, as if they are somehow being disloyal to their adoptive parents. Foster children may be angry with the parents who placed them in foster care, and equally resentful of their foster parents' attempts to care for them.

If you have been adopted, or are in a foster family, you may feel a real sense of grief—a longing for your birth parents and a sadness that your dream of a "perfect" family has not been realized. You may wish for answers to questions like "Why didn't they want me?" and "What would have happened if they had kept me?" and yet be afraid of what the answers to those questions would be.

These feelings and emotions are all very normal and natural. There are some practical steps that you can take to help you manage these emotions, without denying them or letting them manage you.

## Managing anger

Anger can be a harsh feeling, swirling up suddenly and unexpectedly. As you grow older, you will begin to recognize the things that make you most angry. You will begin to see certain patterns in the times when you feel angry, and understand the areas where you are most sensitive.

**Do you recognize the situations that make you feel angry?**

But it is important to do more than understand what makes you angry. You must also be able to manage your anger. Anger can create a tremendous amount of energy—you want to be able to direct that energy into a positive, rather than negative, force.

One outlet may be physical activity. Sports are a great way to channel energy, whether you choose a team sport like football, soccer, or field hockey or a competitive sport like swimming or running. When you are engaged in a vigorous sport, your body releases certain chemicals, called endorphins, which help you feel better.

Anger is also released when it is spoken out loud. This

does not mean that you should let go of your anger in a burst of shouting or cursing. It does mean that you should be honest about your feelings, and not pretend to be happy when you are really angry. It is okay to tell someone—a parent, a friend—"It really makes me angry when you . . . " or "It made me mad that you decided to. . . . " It can be frightening to think about speaking a strong feeling like anger out loud, and it can take courage to let someone know that they hurt you. But sharing your feelings in this way, being honest about what makes you angry or what hurt you in the past, helps others to understand how they can better care for you and care about you in the future.

If the thought of speaking your anger out loud seems overwhelming right now, you may wish to write down your feelings instead. Pretend that you are writing a letter—to your birth parent, to your adoptive or foster parent, to whoever has made you angry—and put down on paper what they have done that has been hurtful to you. Be as honest as you want

**Would it be easier to tell someone how you feel, or put your feelings in a letter?**

to. You never need to send that letter, unless you want to. Or keep a journal or diary, and record what you are feeling. Writing down your anger can be a powerful way to release the emotion honestly, without trying to shove it back inside and pretend it doesn't exist, and can provide you with greater understanding of the times and events that trigger angry feelings.

If you are angry at your birth parents, one additional step that may be helpful is to learn as much as you can about the reasons why they felt they were unable to care for you. Understanding their circumstances, while not excusing them, may help you better appreciate that their decision was not taken lightly but was done in the honest hope that you would have a better life elsewhere.

**When the problems and stress of life become overwhelming, it is possible to find relief from feelings of depression by turning to friends and the activities that make us happy.**

## Dealing with depression

Depression can be a deadly emotion, robbing you of energy and enthusiasm. It is important to recognize depression and to take steps to manage it.

Depression is a feeling of deep and lasting sadness, a sense of disappointment in life. For adopted and foster children, this feeling often follows significant events or holidays—a birthday, Mother's Day or Father's Day—or may be triggered by a memory, a remark, or even something seemingly unrelated.

Depression's greatest power is its ability to turn the world into a gray place, as if it were shutting doors and windows and closing out all the sources of light. It is important to fight back, to not allow yourself to be closed into a sad place. The first and best thing you can do is to force yourself to keep moving, to continue to do the things that normally make you happy, even when you don't want to. If you enjoy being outdoors, go outside for a walk or a run. If you feel better with friends, call them and arrange to meet somewhere. The important thing is to hold on to the things that make you happy and continue to do them, even when your energy level is low.

Remember that this feeling, like all feelings, is temporary. The situation that caused you to feel sad is also temporary. If you are feeling helpless because of the actions of the adults in your life, remember that you, too, will soon be an adult and be able to make your own decisions about where and how you want to live. While you are not responsible for the circumstances of your life, you are responsible for how you react to them. Choose not to be overwhelmed, but instead find the things that make you happy and hold onto them. Look for friends, for people who make you feel good about yourself, and spend time with them.

## Overcoming fear

The unknown can be a source of great anxiety and stress, and for adopted and foster children, there is much that is unknown. For adopted children, much of that which is unknown lies in the past. For foster children, it is the future that often contains a lot of question marks.

In either case, it is possible to master your fears, and to handle the stress that comes with change or uncertainty. The first step is to admit to being frightened—to examine what it is that worries you in the open, rather than keeping it bottled inside. Talk to a friend, a counselor, to someone you trust about whatever is worrying you or making you feel frightened. If you don't feel comfortable sharing your fears

> **Do you keep your feelings bottled up, or talk about them?**

out loud, write them down. Put your fears on paper and then think about the reasons why this particular fear bothers you.

Admitting your fears is the first step to confronting them and, eventually, conquering them. At times, you may feel uncomfortable or uneasy about a particular situation, event, or possibility, and when you speak it out loud or write it on paper, you will begin to understand the fear better. A fear may seem large and unmanageable until you begin to talk about it, and then you find that it gradually grows smaller and easier to handle.

If you are frightened of another new move, another change, talk about or write about the reasons why this change worries you. Once you have thought about each possibility, you can think about steps to handle them, one by one. If you are worried about an upcoming meeting with a birth parent, you can examine each possible outcome of that visit, and then come up with a plan to handle each different possibility. If you are frightened that your foster family may not keep you, talk with someone you trust who can help—a social worker or case worker, a counselor, or your foster parents. Be honest about your feelings. Let them know your wishes. Be clear with yourself and others, so that they can understand your feelings and, if possible, take steps to help you.

The most important thing to remember, as you deal with the many feelings wrapped up in being adopted or being in a foster family, is that you are not alone. There are many people, and many organizations, who wish to help you. Some of these resources are listed at the end of this book.

A family is much more than a group of adults and children who share the same genes. A family is created when a circle of people is joined with one common goal—to love and care for each other. Families may be shaped by many different factors, but regardless of what

**A healthy, happy family depends on a lot more than being related by blood. The bonds of caring and communication can help families raising an adopted or foster child face future challenges as a team.**

challenges they face, the bonds they share are more than simply flesh and blood. A "real" family is the one that nurtures and supports each person in it. When this happens, the circumstances that first brought that family together are merely the beginning of a story that is still unfolding.

# Glossary

**Adoption** – the legal right given to a parent or parents to raise a child as their own, even though they are not the birth parents of the child.

**Birth parent** – a child's natural parent, to whom they are related by blood.

**Ethnic background** – characteristics, such as appearance, that a particular race or group of people have in common.

**Foster** – to help something grow or develop.

**Foster children** – children who live with a foster family on a temporary basis, when their birth parents cannot care for them.

**Foster family** – a family made up of foster children and foster parents, an arrangement that ideally exists for a short period of time until foster children can be adopted or returned to their birth parents.

**Foster parents** – parents who give foster children a safe place to live when their own parents are unable to care for them.

**International adoption** – an adoption of a child in one country by parents in another country.

**Life book** – a book kept by an adopted or foster child to record the facts, background, and events that made them who they are.

**Non-identifying information** – basic facts about a birth mother—such as health, appearance, and religious background—that an adoption agency will have on record.

**Private adoption** – an adoption arranged through a attorney, doctor, or other private contact.

**Transethnic** or **transracial adoption** – an adoption in which the child is of a different race or ethnic background than their adoptive parents.

# Further Reading

**Books:**

Burlingham-Brown, Barbara. *Why Didn't She Keep Me? Answers to the Questions Every Adopted Child Asks*. South Bend, IN: Langford Books, 1994.

Gabel, Susan. *Filling in the Blanks: A Guided Look at Growing Up Adopted*. Fort Wayne, IN: Perspectives Press, 1988.

Gravelle, Karen and Fischer, Susan. *Where Are My Birth Parents? A Guide for Teenage Adoptees*. New York: Walker & Company, 1993.

Krementz, Jill. *How It Feels to Be Adopted*. New York: Alfred A. Knopf, 1983.

Lowry, Lois. *Find a Stranger, Say Goodbye*. Boston: Houghton Mifflin, 1978.

Nixon, Joan Lowery. *Caught in the Act*. New York: Bantam Books, 1988.

Okimoto, Jean Davies. *Molly by any Other Name*. New York: Scholastic Inc., 1990.

# Further Reading

**Web Sites:**

General information about adoption

www.adopt.org

www.adoptinfo.net

www.adoptioncrossroads.org

www.adoptionnetwork.org

www.hannahandhermama.com

www.kidshealth.org

www.rosieodonnell.com

www.teenadoptees.freeservers.com

International adoptions

www.childbook.com
  *contains information about summer culture camps for children adopted from China*

www.connections-india.com
  *information for families with children adopted from India*

www.fcvn.org
  *information for families with children from Vietnam*

www.frua.org
  *focuses on families with Russian and Ukranian children*

www.fwcc.org
  *resource for families with children from China*

# Index

# About the Author

**Heather Lehr Wagner** is a writer and editor. She is the author of several books for teens, including *Understanding and Coping with Divorce* and *Dealing with Terminal Illness in the Family* in the Focus on Family Matters series.

# About the Editor

**Marvin Rosen** is a licensed clinical psychologist who practices in Media, Pennsylvania. He received his doctorate degree from the University of Pennsylvania in 1961. Since 1963, he has worked with intellectually and emotionally challenged people at Elwyn, Inc. in Pennsylvania, with clinical, administrative, research, and training responsibilities. He also conducts a private practice of psychology. Dr. Rosen has taught psychology at the University of Pennsylvania, Bryn Mawr College, and West Chester University. He has written or edited seven book and numerous professional articles in the areas of psychology, rehabilitation, emotional disturbance, and mental retardation.